I0459449

# THE UGLY TRUTH BEHIND A BEAUTIFUL FACE

A Journey of Pain, Purpose, and Healing

Rodlyn Wilson

THE UGLY TRUTH BEHIND A BEAUTIFUL FACE

Copyright © 2025 All rights reserved— Rodlyn Wilson

No part of this book may be reproduced or transmitted in any form or by any means, graphic, electronic, or mechanical, including photocopying, recording, taping, or by an information storage retrieval system without the written permission of the publisher. The contents and cover of this book may not be reproduced in whole or in part in any form without the express written permission of the author or B.O.Y. Enterprises, Inc.

Please direct all copyright inquiries to:

rodlynprince@yahoo.com

Paperback ISBN: 978-1-955605-92-2

Cover Design: Rodlyn Wilson

Interior Design: B.O.Y. Enterprises, Inc.

Printed in the United States.

## Dedication

To my two sons... my greatest gifts, my reasons for pushing forward, and the reminders that God's love never fails.

To my husband... my answered prayer and proof that love can be redeemed.

And to every woman who has ever felt unseen, unheard, or unworthy... this is for you. May you find your reflection in these words and know that your beauty was never lost, only waiting to be uncovered.

# Table of Contents

# Preface – My Why

There comes a moment in every life when silence starts to feel heavier than the truth. For years, I carried my story in pieces — fragments of pain, shame, joy, and redemption — never realizing that God was writing something far bigger than my brokenness.

The Ugly Truth from a Beautiful Face is not just my testimony. It's my healing. It's for every woman who's smiled through pain, every child who's hidden behind perfection, and every believer who's ever questioned if God still sees them in the dark.

This book is proof that He does. That He can take what was meant to destroy you and turn it into your ministry. That beauty and ashes can coexist — and out of both, something holy can be born.

So, if you're reading this, know this: you're not alone. Healing isn't pretty, but it's powerful. And this… is my journey to becoming whole.

# Introduction

Sometimes God has a way of reminding us exactly who He is. He will place us in situations where the only direction we can look is up—where our strength, our answers, and our peace can come only from Him.

I've learned that having a beautiful face, a nice home, cars, land, or even money does not make us exempt from hardship. Those things can't protect us from heartbreak, betrayal, or being misunderstood. Every single one of us carries what I call an ugly truth—the painful parts of our story that we wish we could hide, the memories that shaped us even when we didn't understand why.

But here's the thing: our ugly truth made us who we are today. We all go through seasons that leave scars—moments when we take on new identities just to survive. We try to imitate the strength, confidence, or perfection we see in others, but

God doesn't bless imitation; He blesses

authenticity. He wants us to take responsibility for our truth, to own it, and to walk in it without shame.

So many of us spend years hiding behind pain, pretending everything is fine, because we don't want the world to see our vulnerability. But there is liberty in owning your story. There is healing in being honest about where you've been.

I'm here to tell you that nothing you've been through was in vain. Every struggle, every mistake, every loss—it all served a purpose. Your testimony can free someone else from their silence.

Maybe you've been divorced, molested, heartbroken, or abandoned. Maybe you've served time in prison or lived through seasons of deep depression. Whatever your story is, that is your truth. And God can use even the ugliest parts of your truth to reveal His beauty through you.

We all fall short, but that doesn't mean we stop living. You are still who God created you to be, even with the bumps in your journey. You are not disqualified because of what you went through—you are qualified because you survived it.

So as you read this book, I pray that my story helps you embrace yours. I pray that you find the courage to stand in your own truth, even when it hurts. Because healing begins where hiding ends.

# Chapter One

## Wearing a Mask: The Hidden Faces We Wear

When the world shut down in 2020, everyone started wearing masks to protect themselves from a virus that could take their breath away. But if we're honest, many of us had been wearing masks long before that—just not the kind you could see.

Some of us wore masks to hide pain. Some of us smiled to cover heartbreak. Some of us dressed up our wounds and called it strength. But no matter how pretty the mask looked, it was only hiding what was hurting underneath. The truth is, the mask doesn't just protect, it suffocates. I learned that the hard way.

### Growing Up Behind the Mask

I grew up as a preacher's kid. My father was a Bishop, my mother the First Lady, and our family was deeply rooted in the church. Ministry wasn't just a calling—it was our lifestyle. If we weren't traveling to sing, we were in Wednesday night prayer or Sunday morning worship. Everyone saw the polished image of a perfect family serving God, but behind the stage lights, there were shadows.

Like so many families, we lived by the rule: *"Whatever goes on in this house stays in this house."* That meant no matter what happened—arguments, tension, or pain—we smiled through it. We looked the part because image mattered. And for me, that lesson ran deep.

I learned how to perform early. I learned how to walk into church smiling after crying the night before. How to clap and sing through heartache. How to hide emotions so well that even I forgot what I truly felt. I was the preacher's daughter; people expected perfection. But what they didn't see was the little girl behind the smile—hurting and confused.

## When Silence Becomes a Prison

At fourteen, something happened that changed me. I was standing in a church hallway when a minister, a man who should've been safe, cornered me and tried to kiss me. I froze. I didn't scream. I didn't tell. I just pushed past him, pretending it didn't happen.

Every Sunday after that, I saw his face. I wanted to say something, but fear told me not to. What would people think? Would they believe me? Would it ruin my father's ministry? So, I stayed silent. And that silence became a prison.

I carried that weight for years; smiling on the outside but dying on the inside. That moment taught

9

me how to live hidden, how to wear the mask even tighter, and how to make pain look like peace. But deep down, the mask was eating away at me. Because what you bury alive doesn't die, it festers. And the longer you hide it, the deeper the infection goes.

## Losing Myself in the Image

As I got older, the mask didn't just stay in the church—it followed me into adulthood. It shaped how I loved, how I trusted, and how I saw myself. I was always trying to be "enough," always performing for approval I didn't even need.

The mask taught me how to fake peace but never how to *find* it. I thought being strong meant pretending. I thought if I looked okay, maybe I would start to feel okay. But pretending didn't heal me, it hardened me.

Behind closed doors, I would cry out to God, asking why I still felt broken when I was doing everything "right." I prayed, served, sang, and smiled—but the little girl inside me was still bleeding. I didn't realize then that every time I chose appearance over honesty, I was pushing myself further from freedom.

## God Sees Beyond the Mask

The beautiful thing about God is that He doesn't stop pursuing us, even when we hide. He saw me when I sat in my room alone, wondering why I felt so empty. He saw the little girl trying to protect herself.

And even when I didn't understand it, He was already preparing a path for my healing. God doesn't heal what we hide, but He waits patiently until we're ready to hand Him our broken pieces.

It took me years to understand that wearing a mask doesn't just hide your pain; it delays your purpose. Because you can't walk in freedom while you're pretending to be someone else. So, God began to peel away my layers, not to shame me, but to *free* me. Each tear, each prayer, each moment of surrender was like another layer falling off. And beneath all the pain, He revealed something I hadn't seen in years...*me*.

## The Hard Work of Taking the Mask Off

Taking off the mask wasn't a single moment; it was a process. It meant facing memories I wanted to forget. It meant admitting that I wasn't okay. It meant choosing truth over comfort. And truth doesn't always feel good. It stings before it heals.

There were nights when I cried until I fell asleep, and mornings when I woke up feeling numb. But every time I whispered, *"God, I can't keep pretending,"* I could feel His presence wrap around me like peace. Healing didn't happen all at once. It came little by little—through prayer, through worship, through counseling, through being honest with myself. Every time I opened my mouth and told the truth, I broke another chain. I realized then that God doesn't remove the mask to expose us—He removes it to free us.

Rodlyn Wilson

Because you can't heal from what you hide.

## Learning to Love the Unmasked Me

When the mask came off, I had to meet the real me, the woman underneath the performance. She was scarred, yes, but she was also strong. She was broken, but she was still here.

God showed me that I didn't need to be perfect to be loved. I didn't need to have it all together to be chosen. I just needed to be *real*. And the more I accepted who I was, the more I understood who God was. He was never impressed by the version of me that looked polished—He loved the version that was honest, messy, and trying her best. I used to think freedom came from control, but now I know freedom comes from surrender.

## Freedom Looks Good on You

Looking back, I realize that the girl behind the mask wasn't weak; she was just trying to survive. But the woman I am now? She's thriving. I learned that strength isn't pretending to have it all together. Real strength is admitting when you don't. It's choosing to heal instead of hide. It's being vulnerable enough to let God rebuild you from the inside out.

The truth is, we all wear masks at some point. But at some point, we all have to take them off. So, if you're reading this, maybe it's your time. Maybe this is your moment to stop pretending and start healing. Because freedom looks good on you, and it's been waiting for you all along.

**Closing Prayer**

Lord, thank You for showing me the mask I used to wear and for meeting me when I was hiding. Give me courage to step out of performance and into honesty, even when it's hard. Help me to be seen for who I truly am and to find my worth in You, not in approval or appearances. Heal the places that made me pretend and teach me to walk in authenticity. In Jesus' name, Amen.

## Chapter Two

*Seeing Myself Through God's Eyes*

Taking off the mask was only the beginning. Once the layers of pretense were gone, I was forced to face what I had been avoiding for years—the pain itself. You see, removing the mask doesn't automatically make you healed. It just makes you ready.

Ready to feel.

Ready to forgive.

Ready to start doing the real work.

And for me, that next step wasn't easy. Because once I stopped pretending, all the pain I had buried began to rise to the surface. The little girl I silenced for years finally started to speak. And her voice changed everything.

### The Reflection in the Mirror

Self-image, what we see when we look in the

mirror, is shaped long before we ever understand what beauty truly means. It's not just about what's on the outside; it's about what we believe about ourselves deep within—our worth, our identity, and our value. But for many of us, that image has been shaped by what *other people* said about us, not what God said.

I still remember being five years old when my parents realized I could sing. They would take me to churches and events, and people would say, *"That little girl has a beautiful voice!"* One day, I stood backstage at a concert, palms sweating, heart racing, about to sing *"Who's Gonna Tell the Child About Jesus."*

The crowd was packed from wall to wall. My mother leaned over, looked me in the eyes, and whispered gently, *"Stop crying, baby. Everything will be okay."* That was the first time I questioned myself: *Am I good enough? What if I mess up? What will they think of me?* I didn't know it then, but that was the beginning of a lifelong struggle with self-image.

## The Lies That Shape Us

When I got to school, those questions only got louder. I remember walking through the hallways hearing kids whisper about my clothes, my shoes, my hair. Back then, if you weren't wearing the "right" brands—FUBU, Nike, Sean John, you were a target. Then came the jokes.

One boy once shouted across class, *"What has a flat surface? Rodlyn's chest!"* The whole room erupted in laughter. I felt my face burn as I fought back tears. From that day on, I wore jackets and sweatshirts to hide myself. I was ashamed of the body God gave me.

Another time, kids called me "Dumbo" because of my ears, saying I could fly away. So, I wore my hair down to hide what they called flaws. Little by little, I started believing their words over God's truth. And then came the comment that cut the deepest:

*"You're cute to be a dark-skinned girl."*

Those words stung in a way I can't explain. It was as if my beauty came with conditions, as if my skin tone determined my value. I didn't have a name for it back then, but I later learned it was colorism. And colorism plants seeds of shame that grow into lifelong insecurity if they're never uprooted.

One day, I remember asking my mom for the bottle of Clorox, pretending I needed it to clean. I took it into the bathroom, desperate and broken, and started scrubbing my skin with it, hoping I could make myself lighter. That's how deeply I wanted to feel *beautiful*. Looking back now, I see that moment for what it was; an attack on my identity. The enemy knew that if he could make me hate myself, he could distract me from my purpose. Because when you don't know who you are, you'll spend your life trying to become what everyone else wants you to be.

**The Truth About Beauty**

Genesis 1:27 says, *"So God created man in His own*

*image; in the image of God He created him."* That means everything about me...my skin, my smile, my laugh, and my body was made with intention. God didn't make a mistake when He made me. But for years, I believed He did.

As I got older, I began noticing how society glorified a specific kind of beauty: small waist, big hips, flawless face. If you didn't fit the mold, you were made to feel invisible. I watched women alter their bodies and risk their lives for the validation I was still chasing in silence. I remember saving up money for a procedure I thought would finally make me feel confident. But deep down, I knew the surgery wouldn't fix what was broken inside, it would only decorate the pain. God had to teach me that *beauty without peace is just decoration.* And real peace starts when you stop asking, *"What's wrong with me?"* and start declaring, *"God made me on purpose."*

## Healing the Girl in the Mirror

Healing my self-image didn't happen overnight. It took prayer, tears, therapy, and  surrender. I had to stand in front of the mirror and tell myself the truth. I was worthy, beautiful, and enough, not because of the world's approval, but because of God's design. I started thanking God for what I used to complain about—my skin, my features, my story. And every time I did, a piece of that old shame fell away.

Now, when I look in the mirror, I don't see a girl who needs to be fixed. I see a woman who has been *redeemed.* I still have moments when the old thoughts try to creep back in. But now, I remind myself: *I am fearfully and wonderfully made. My dark skin is beautiful. My scars are beautiful. My story is beautiful.* And so is yours.

## Becoming Who I Was Always Meant to Be

As I grew older, I realized something powerful. If the enemy could get me to question my worth as a little girl, he could influence the choices I made as a woman. Every insecurity I carried became a doorway for broken love to enter my life. Every lie I believed about myself shaped the kind of love I accepted. I thought I needed to earn love, to work for affection, and prove that I was enough.

So, I let people stay who only wanted parts of me because I was afraid the whole me wouldn't be enough. I confused attention for love. I mistook control for care. I accepted pain because I thought it was my portion. But what I didn't realize was that I was chasing love from a place of unhealed wounds. The truth is, when you don't heal what hurt you, you'll keep attracting what broke you.

## Seeing the Bigger Picture

As I began to mature in faith, God started showing me that my struggles with self-image weren't just about how I saw myself in the mirror — they were reflections of something much deeper. My pain didn't start with the teasing or the rejection. It started long

19

before that, in moments I had buried so deep I didn't even remember how much they shaped me.

God began to whisper to my spirit, *"It's time to go deeper."* And that's what true healing requires honesty. Because until you face the parts of your story that still bleed, you'll keep putting bandages over what needs surgery. The mirror could no longer fix what was broken beneath the surface. The affirmations were no longer enough. The little girl in me was still crying for help; and this time, I was finally ready to listen.

By the time I began to see myself through God's eyes, I started realizing that beauty and confidence alone weren't the full picture. Something deeper was still broken. Because healing your reflection doesn't mean you've healed your foundation.

The truth is, there were still parts of me that hadn't been touched by healing yet; wounds I had buried so deep that I convinced myself they didn't exist anymore. But God has a way of shining light in the darkest corners of our hearts. And when He does, it's never to shame us. It's to set us free.

As I stood at this new crossroads in my life, I felt God whisper, *"Now, let's deal with what's underneath."* That's when I realized that before I could truly love myself, before I could forgive others, and before I could walk fully in purpose, I had to confront the one thing I spent my whole life running from: my trauma. Because you can't heal what you refuse to face. And for the first time, I was ready to face it.

## Closing Prayer

Lord, thank You for reminding me that I was made on purpose and in Your image. Help me to see my reflection the way You see me beloved, chosen, and whole. Replace the lies about my worth with Your truth and restore the beauty You planted inside me.

Teach me to speak life over myself and to honor the body and soul You gave me. In Jesus' name, Amen.

# Chapter Three

## Traumatic Experiences

### When Pain Becomes a Part of You

Trauma is a word that holds so much weight. It's more than something that happens to you, it's something that changes you. It shapes how you see yourself, how you love, how you trust, and how you move through the world. A traumatic experience is any moment that causes physical, emotional, or spiritual harm. It leaves behind invisible bruises that no one can see, but that you feel every single day. Those wounds may fade from memory, but they never really disappear. They live beneath the surface until you decide to face them.

We often don't realize how much pain from our childhood follows us into adulthood. When you've been abused, neglected, abandoned, or betrayed, those experiences don't just vanish with time. They sink deep into your soul, whispering lies that shape your identity. Lies like: *You're not enough. You're unlovable. You'll never be whole again.* But the truth is, those lies don't come from God.

## The God Who Holds You in the Storm

Isaiah 41:10 reminds us, *"Fear not, for I am with you; be not dismayed, for I am your God. I will strengthen you and help you; I will uphold you with My righteous right hand."* Even in our darkest moments, God is still holding us, even when we can't feel His hand. Looking back now, I can see how the storms I went through were not meant to break me, but to build me. But in those moments, all I could see was pain.

When I was a little girl, I didn't have the words to describe what was happening to me. I went through things that no child should ever have to experience; moments that left me feeling dirty, ashamed, and broken. I was sexually abused by someone who should have been a protector, not a predator.

The innocence that was stolen from me left behind a silence so loud it followed me for years. I thought it was my fault. I thought maybe if I had done something differently, it wouldn't have happened. That's the lie trauma tells you — that you deserved it. But you didn't. And I didn't. What happened to me was not a reflection of who I was. It was a reflection of someone else's brokenness.

## The Weight of Silence

I carried that secret like a brick on my chest. I smiled on the outside while suffocating inside. I became a master at pretending everything was okay. But the silence was heavy, and the guilt was even heavier. As I got older, the pain didn't go away — it just changed form. The little girl who was afraid to speak became the woman who doubted her worth. The shame turned into low self- esteem, anxiety, depression, and even thoughts of suicide. I would cry at night, wondering if life would ever feel normal again.

But what I didn't understand then was that the sadness I felt wasn't just emotion. It was *trauma speaking through me.* The devil loves to twist trauma to make you doubt God's love. He did the same thing to Eve in Genesis 3. He made her question what God had already said. *"Did God really say...?"* he whispered.

And that's what trauma does, it makes you question everything. It makes you wonder, *"If God loved me, why did this happen?"* or *"Where was He when I was crying out for help?"* But the truth is, He was right there. He never left. He was crying when I cried, hurting when I hurt, waiting for the day I'd stop running and let Him heal me.

## The Road to Recovery

It took me years to understand that my trauma didn't disqualify me; it defined my ministry. The pain that almost destroyed me became the very thing God used to shape my purpose. But before that revelation came healing, and healing came with confrontation. I had to stop avoiding my memories and start processing them. I had to sit with my younger self — that scared, silent little girl — and tell her, *"It wasn't your fault."* I had to face my feelings instead of numbing them, and I had to let God enter the places I had locked Him out of.

Healing didn't happen overnight. There were tears, triggers, counseling sessions, and prayers that ended in silence. But each step forward, no matter how small, was progress. God began showing me that my pain had purpose. The same girl who once felt unworthy would one day tell her story so another woman could find freedom.

## From Pain to Purpose

There's a phrase I hold onto now: *"There's purpose behind the pain."* For so long, I thought my trauma was punishment from God. I thought He was angry with me, that I had done something wrong. But now I see it differently. God wasn't punishing me. He was preparing me. He was refining me in the fire so that when I came out, I could help others find warmth in their own storms. Every scar became evidence of survival, every tear became a testimony.

What the enemy meant for evil, God truly turned for good. Now I understand why the enemy attacked me so young, because he saw the woman I would become. He knew that if I ever healed, I'd be dangerous to the kingdom of darkness. And he was right. Because now, I don't just speak from pain. I speak from *power!*

## Healing Is a Process

Healing from trauma isn't about forgetting what happened. It's about releasing its power over you. It's about giving God permission to turn your wounds into wisdom. You can't heal what you keep hiding. And you can't walk in freedom if you keep living in fear. Healing means asking yourself hard questions:

- What happened to me?

- How did it shape the way I see myself?

- What do I still need to release?

The answers may hurt, but they will also set you free. You don't have to carry the shame anymore. You don't have to keep reliving the pain. You can release it, because healing belongs to you.

As I began facing my trauma, something shifted inside me. I realized that healing wasn't just about forgiving others. It was about forgiving myself. The little girl inside of me had been waiting for someone to tell her, *"You're safe now. You can rest."*

And that's what God did. He gave me permission to rest in His safety. He took my pain and turned it into peace. He began leading me through a journey of *inner healing;* teaching me how to pray through my pain, forgive through my tears, and walk in freedom even when my heart still ached. I didn't know it then, but the process I was about to enter would change my life forever. Because inner healing isn't just recovery...it's rebirth.

## Closing Prayer

*Lord, thank You for holding me through the pain I could not carry alone. Meet me in every wound and bring the healing only You can give. Help me to release the shame and the lies trauma whispered and to receive Your truth about who I am. Give me courage to keep walking toward recovery and to trust You with the pieces I cannot fix. In Jesus' name, Amen.*

## Chapter Four

## Covering Your Wound but Still Bleeding: Learning to Heal the Right Way

We all know what it's like to get a cut. You clean it, bandage it, and give it time. But if you cover it too quickly or never treat the infection underneath, it festers. It may look fine on the outside, but inside it's still bleeding.

That's exactly how I lived for years, walking around with emotional wounds that looked covered, but underneath, I was still hurting. I was smiling, singing, showing up for everyone, but bleeding on the inside where no one could see.

### When Love Turns into Loss

At 12 years old, I lost my innocence to someone much older; an 18-year-old who convinced me that what we were doing was love. "If you love me, you'll do this," he said. I was a child who didn't yet understand manipulation, and so I believed him. I believed that giving myself would finally mean I was loved. But love doesn't leave you ashamed. Love doesn't steal your childhood. Because I didn't deal with it, history repeated itself at 14, this time with a 34-year-old man. The wound that was never healed reopened all over again.

## Bleeding in Silence

When my parents found out, the police were called. Everyone in the community heard about it. At school, kids whispered behind my back and called me names: "liar," "snitch." They made me feel like I was the problem. I wasn't just wounded. I was bleeding.

I began coping the only way I knew how. I started cutting my wrists; not because I wanted to die, but because I didn't know how else to silence the pain that was screaming inside me. The physical pain felt easier to control than the emotional one. I wore long sleeves to hide the scars, even from my parents.

When you don't treat the root of your pain, it infects your soul. You start believing you're unworthy, broken beyond repair, or too far gone for God to fix. But the enemy is a liar. Jesus said in John 10:10, *"The thief comes only to steal and kill and destroy. I came that they may have life, and have it abundantly."*

I now know that every cut I made, every tear I cried, and every moment I felt forgotten, God saw it all. Even in my darkest moments, He never left me. I just didn't know how to reach for Him yet.

Covering our wounds might make us look strong on the outside, but true healing starts when we're honest — first with ourselves, then with God, and then with the people who love us. Healing begins when we stop pretending the wound isn't there. When I finally opened up and got help, it wasn't easy. I had to relive moments that hurt to even think about. But healing required honesty. And honesty led me to freedom.

## The Invitation to Healing

If you're walking around today with unhealed pain, I want you to know this: You cannot heal what you keep hiding. You have to speak it. Pray about it. Ask for help. You don't have to carry the shame of what happened to you because shame was never yours to carry in the first place.

Yes, you may still have scars. But scars aren't signs of weakness — they're evidence that God healed you. Psalm 147:3 says, "He heals the brokenhearted and binds up their wounds." Let Him bind yours. Don't just cover it this time, let Him heal it.

Finally telling the truth about my pain was only the beginning. When I uncovered the wounds, I expected immediate relief, but what I felt instead was a flood of emotions I had buried for years. It was overwhelming. The same girl who had been so good at pretending was now standing in the middle of her truth and it felt heavier than ever. That heaviness brought me to the darkest place I had ever been.

## Closing Prayer

Lord, thank You for uncovering the wounds I covered for so long. Teach me not to wrap them tighter but to bring them to You for healing. Give me the humility to ask for help and the strength to be honest about what I need. Heal the infection of silence and shame and bind up what is broken with Your grace. In Jesus' name, Amen.

# Chapter Five

## Suicide: The Battle for My Life

Life can be heavy. Sometimes, it can feel so heavy you feel like you're drowning beneath it. You smile, you go to school, you go to church, you post happy pictures online, but inside, you're gasping for air. I know that feeling intimately.

Suicide is not just a statistic; it's a dark, quiet place too many people find themselves in. According to national data, one person dies by suicide every 40 seconds. But when you're the one living through it, those numbers don't matter. What matters is the ache in your chest, the voices in your head, and the hopelessness you can't shake.

I was only 14 years old when I felt like the world would be better off without me. A child, and yet my heart carried more grief than it knew what to do with. Everything you've read in the previous chapters — the trauma, the shame, the bullying, the silence — it built up inside of me like a storm. On the outside, I was the preacher's kid, the girl with the voice, the smile, the potential. On the inside, I was a girl who believed she had failed at life before it even began.

I would sit in my room and cry silently into my pillow. Sometimes I wouldn't eat. Sometimes I wouldn't speak for days. My thoughts became darker with every passing moment.

They don't really love you.

You're just a burden.

You're damaged goods.

You should just end it.

Those were the whispers I heard, over and over. I didn't understand it then, but now I know that was spiritual warfare. The enemy knew that God had a plan for my life. He knew that one day, I'd be writing this book to set others free. And if he could destroy me before I discovered my purpose, he would.

## God's Whisper in the Darkness

I remember trying to take pills. I remember sitting with a blade, staring at my wrist, thinking, I just want the pain to stop. I didn't really want to die. I wanted relief.

### But God had other plans.

It was a Sunday night. The house was quiet, but inside me everything was loud. My mind felt like a war zone; thoughts of shame, hopelessness, and death pounding against my skull. I wasn't looking for attention. I wasn't being dramatic. I just wanted the pain to stop. And in that dark room, I heard it — a whisper: *"Stop."* It wasn't my own voice. It was the Holy Spirit. I didn't understand it then, but God was intervening.


## The Moment Everything Changed

My mom woke up in the middle of the night as if something had nudged her awake. She found me crying silently. For weeks, she'd seen I wasn't myself. I wasn't eating, talking, or smiling. That night, she didn't hesitate. "Get dressed," she said. "We're going to the hospital."

I can still smell the antiseptic of the emergency room. The lights were harsh, white, and cold. Nurses moved briskly down the halls while my parents spoke in hushed voices with the doctor. Even without hearing their words, I could feel their fear.

The psychiatrist entered, sat down, and looked at me with gentle eyes.

"Do you feel like hurting yourself?" he asked softly.

I couldn't speak, so I nodded.

"Do you want to be here?" he asked again.

I nodded again, though inside I was screaming, *I don't want to die. I just don't know how to live.*

That's when they made the decision. I was going to be admitted for emergency treatment. For the first time, I saw my parents not just as protectors, but as people who were terrified to lose me.

## Chapter Six
### The Mental Institution: Finding God in the Locked Places

When you hear the words *mental institution,* most people think of something scary, a place for "other people," a place whispered about but never seen. I never imagined that at 14 years old, I'd be admitted to one. I was the preacher's kid. The girl with the bright smile. The singer with big dreams. But none of that kept me from reaching my breaking point and ending up in a mental institution.

### Inside the Walls

They transported me to the mental health facility. As the van pulled away, I looked out the window — streetlights blurred past like streaks of gold. I thought about my friends, school, church, and how people would look at me if they knew. I wondered if God still saw me at all.

When we arrived, the heavy click of the door locking behind me echoed in my chest. They took my shoelaces, my belt, anything that could harm me. I felt stripped of everything, even my identity.

The ward was divided: boys on one side, girls on the other. The walls were a dull cream; the floors, a faded gray. It smelled like disinfectant and cafeteria food. The beds were thin, the blankets scratchy. There was no softness anywhere — not in the light, not in the rules.

## Life Behind Locked Doors

Every day was structured down to the minute.

6:30 a.m. — wake up.
7:00 — breakfast.
9:00 — group therapy.
11:00 — schoolwork.
Noon — lunch.
1:00 — more therapy.
8:00 — free time.
9:00 — lights out.

The routine felt like prison, but in a strange way, it gave me something I hadn't had in a long time: *structure*. In group sessions, we sat in circles sharing our stories. For the first time, I realized I wasn't alone.

There was Ashley — 13 years old, a mother because her father had raped her. Her pain was unthinkable. She told us how she mixed Clorox in her baby's formula because she didn't want to remember her trauma. She had tried to drive off a bridge.

Then there was Rachel, who had been raped by a stranger on her way home from school. She said she felt like her soul left her body. She cut herself just to feel something again.

Listening to their stories, something shifted inside me. I realized pain doesn't discriminate against everyone. We were all broken in different ways, all bleeding beneath invisible bandages.

## Finding God in the Unlikely Place

There were moments of fear, lockdowns when someone tried to hurt themselves, the sound of keys jangling at night, kids crying in the hallway. But there were also moments of connection. We played puzzles, watched TV, and talked about our dreams. And in those small, quiet moments, I began to sense God's presence again. He was there, in the counselor who listened without judgment, in the nurse who prayed under her breath before every shift, in the routine that forced my heart to slow down and breathe.

Even behind locked doors, God was still unlocking something inside of me.

Psalm 139:8 says, *"If I make my bed in the depths, You are there."*

That scripture became real to me in that place. Even when I felt unreachable, He found me.

## Learning That Healing Takes Time

I spent about a month in the institution. When I left, I wasn't "fixed" — but I was alive. I had hope again.

Going to a mental hospital isn't shameful. It's brave. It's saying, "I need help, and I'm worth saving." That experience didn't just save my life — it began to rebuild it. I learned that healing is a process. That faith and therapy can work together. That even in sterile, cold, locked-down places, God can still whisper peace.

If you're reading this and you're struggling, please know this: you are not weak. You are not crazy. You are not alone. There is help. There is hope. And there is a God who still sees you.

## The Beauty Hidden in the Breaking

When I left the institution, I didn't walk out completely healed — I walked out *becoming*. Every scar, every tear, and every moment of silence became a piece of something sacred that God was forming in me. For the first time, I realized that being broken didn't mean I was useless. It meant I was being reshaped.

## Breaking the Stigma

In the Black church, we don't talk about suicide enough. We talk about prayer, we talk about fasting, we talk about faith — and all of that is powerful — but we don't always talk about the importance of mental health.

We don't talk about the little girl sitting in the pew who's silently planning her funeral. We don't talk about how depression can sit next to you in the choir stand while you're singing God's praises.

But it's real. And I was living it.


## Prayer and a Plan

As women especially, we're often expected to be strong, to pray it away, to keep going. But strength doesn't mean silence. Strength is knowing when you need help.

That's why I advocate for both God's help and professional help. God gave doctors, therapists, and counselors their gifts for a reason. Sometimes you need prayer and a plan. Sometimes you need a scripture and a psychiatrist. And there is no shame in that.

Looking back, I can see how God orchestrated every step to keep me alive. He allowed my mom to wake up. He allowed the doctor to see through my silence. He allowed me to be in a place where I could start the healing process.

When you're in that dark place, it feels like no one understands. You feel alone, guilty, and ashamed. You think you're weak because you're tired. But you're not weak — you're human. And God still loves you. Isaiah 41:10 says it again: "So do not fear, for I am with you; do not be dismayed, for I am your God. I will strengthen you and help you; I will uphold you with my righteous right hand." He upheld me even when I didn't want to be upheld.

## Purpose Louder than Pain

Today, I can say with confidence: suicide didn't win. Depression didn't win. The enemy didn't win. God won. If you are reading this and you are in that dark place, please know this...your story isn't over. You are not a mistake. You are not a burden. And you are not beyond God's reach. Your pain may be loud right now, but so is your purpose.

## Closing Prayer

Lord, thank You for being with me in the rooms I thought You'd never enter. Thank You for the doctors, nurses, and counselors You used to help me when I couldn't help myself. Remind me — and anyone reading this — that seeking help is not a sign of weakness but of wisdom. May every place that once felt locked become a testimony of Your freedom. In Jesus' name, Amen.

## Chapter Seven
## Finding the Blessing in Brokenness – When the Pieces Begin to Shine

Brokenness. It's a word that makes most people uncomfortable. It sounds final, like something that can't be repaired. But I've learned that brokenness isn't the end. It's often the beginning of everything God wants to do in you. When we think of something broken, we think of something disposable — a shattered cup, a cracked mirror. But in God's hands, broken pieces still have purpose.

### The Day I Saw Brokenness Differently

As a little girl, I was a tomboy who loved basketball. One day, while playing a game of one- on- one, a friend went up for the ball and came down hard on her arm. The snap was sharp and final. She screamed, tears pouring down her face. Months later, after surgery and a cast, her arm healed, but it left a scar. That scar told a story: not of defeat, but of recovery. God used that memory to teach me that our scars are not signs of weakness. They are reminders that we were once broken but God made us whole again.

## The Master Restorer

When I think about healing, I think of restoration. To restore furniture, you must strip away the old layers, sand down the rough edges, and refinish it anew. That's what God does in us. When He sees anger, shame, or bitterness built up over time, He begins to strip those layers away — not to harm us, but to heal us.

It's not comfortable. It's not quick. But it's necessary. Because once He's finished, what's left is stronger, purer, and more beautiful than before. Isaiah 61:3 says, "To bestow on them a crown of beauty instead of ashes, the oil of joy instead of mourning." God doesn't throw away the damaged. He redeems it.

One of my favorite songs growing up was *"The Potter Wants to Put You Back Together Again."* I didn't understand it until life broke me. God is the Potter. We are the clay. When the potter sees cracks in the pot, he doesn't discard it — he breaks it down, moistens it, and reshapes it. That breaking isn't punishment; it's preparation.

Isaiah 64:8 says, *"Yet you, Lord, are our Father. We are the clay, You are the potter; we are all the work of Your hand."*

When God allows your life to come apart, it's not because He's done with you — it's because He's forming something new.

## The Blessing Hidden in the Breaking

For years, I asked God, "Why me?" Why the abuse? Why the depression? Why the hospitalization? But now I understand: every piece of my brokenness carried a blessing. My pain birthed compassion. My trauma birthed a testimony. My scars birthed purpose. Romans 8:28 reminds us, "All things work together for good to those who love God." Even the broken things. Even the bruised things. Even *you*.

One night after leaving the institution, I lay awake asking God, "Why did I have to go through all of that?" And I felt Him whisper:

*"Because someone needs to see that you can break and still be beautiful."*

Tears filled my eyes. For the first time, I didn't feel cursed by my past, I felt called. That night, I realized that my pain was not punishment. It was preparation.

## The Light That Shines Through the Cracks

There's a Japanese art called *Kintsugi,* meaning "golden repair." When pottery breaks, they fill the cracks with gold, making the piece more beautiful than before. That's what God does with us. He fills our cracks with His glory. Our brokenness becomes the very place where His light shines brightest. 2 Corinthians 4:7 says, "But we have this treasure in jars of clay, to show that this all- surpassing power is from God and not from us." Our cracks reveal His power.

## Closing Prayer

Lord, thank You for turning my brokenness into a masterpiece of Your mercy. Thank You for showing me that my scars are proof of Your healing, not my shame. Teach me to see beauty in every place I once tried to hide. Fill my cracks with Your glory and let my story shine for others still in the breaking. In Jesus' name, Amen.

# Chapter Eight
## Forgiveness – The Freedom to Let Go

Forgiveness. It's one of those words that sounds so simple until you actually have to do it. Inner healing doesn't begin with pretending the pain never happened. It begins with facing it, processing it, and then choosing to release it. That's what forgiveness truly is, releasing the weight that was never meant for you to carry.

Forgiveness is more than just saying, *"I'm over it."* It's an act of faith; the courage to hand your hurt to God and trust that He can bring justice, peace, and healing in ways you never could on your own. We talk a lot about praying, fasting, and trusting God, but few people talk about how hard it is to forgive, especially when the person who hurt you never says sorry. I used to think forgiveness meant weakness, like I was letting someone off the hook. But what I've learned is that forgiveness doesn't free them. It frees you.

## The Weight You Can't See

When you hold on to bitterness, resentment, or

anger, it's like walking around with invisible weights tied to your heart. The longer you carry it, the heavier it gets. At first, you think you're fine. You tell yourself you've moved on. But then you hear their name, or someone brings up what happened, and that knot in your stomach tightens again. That's when you realize you're still carrying it. Forgiveness isn't about pretending it didn't hurt. It's about admitting that it did hurt but choosing to let God handle the healing.

I once had a coworker named Sarah when I worked at a call center. She had been holding on to a grudge for years against a woman named Shelia. They had fallen out years before over a man. Sarah had been dating him first, and Shelia, who was supposed to be her friend, started dating the same man behind her back. They stopped speaking after a big argument and hadn't talked for over ten years.

One evening, they ended up at the same dinner party. When Shelia walked in, she saw Sarah sitting across the room whispering to another woman. She immediately assumed Sarah was talking about her and became furious. Unforgiveness will do that because it blinds you to the truth.

Shelia marched across the room and confronted Sarah in front of everyone. But what she didn't know was that Sarah had recently been in a terrible car accident that affected her memory. She wasn't whispering gossip; she was quietly asking the woman next to her who Shelia was because her face looked familiar.

When the woman beside Sarah spoke up and explained the truth, Shelia's face dropped in embarrassment. She realized how wrong she'd been. All those years of bitterness and anger had clouded her judgment. And for what? That's what unforgiveness does. It keeps you stuck in the same moment, even when life has already moved on.

T.D. Jakes once said, *"Unforgiveness is like drinking poison and waiting for the other person to die."* That quote hit me hard the first time I heard it, because I realized I had been drinking that same poison for years.

## When Forgiveness Hit Home

There was a time in my life when God made forgiveness very personal for me. I was going through one of the most painful seasons of my life, a marriage that was falling apart. I loved deeply, I gave everything I had, and still, it ended in heartbreak. I was angry; not just at him, but at myself. I kept replaying every argument, every lie, every broken promise, thinking, *What could I have done differently?*

But the truth is, sometimes it's not about what you could've done. It's about what God is allowing. I wanted to heal, but I couldn't while I was still holding on to resentment. Every time I prayed, I could feel that wall between me and God. And He kept whispering to my heart, *"You can't be free until you forgive."*

I remember crying one night, feeling like my chest was about to explode from the pain. I said, *"God, how do I forgive someone who isn't even sorry?"* And the Holy Spirit spoke so clearly to my heart: *"You forgive them for you — not for them."*

That night, I started the process. I didn't feel healed overnight, but every day I chose to let go a little more. I started praying blessings over the same people who had hurt me. It wasn't easy. Some days I meant it, some days I didn't. But I kept doing it anyway. And you know what happened? The more I prayed, the lighter I felt. Forgiveness didn't change what happened — but it changed me.

## Forgiving Yourself

The hardest person to forgive, though, wasn't anyone else. It was me. I had to forgive myself for staying too long in places where I wasn't valued. For ignoring red flags because I wanted love to work. For letting people take my kindness for weakness. For carrying guilt that God had already forgiven.

Self-forgiveness is part of healing too. Sometimes we beat ourselves up for things that God already forgot about. The Bible says in Micah 7:19, *"You will cast all our sins into the depths of the sea."* If God has already thrown it away, why are you still diving back in to retrieve it? You are not your past. You are not your mistakes. You are not what they said about you. Forgiveness means giving yourself permission to move on — to stop defining yourself by who you were when you were hurting.

## The Power of Letting Go

When you choose forgiveness, you're choosing peace over pain, growth over grudges, and healing over hate. I've learned that forgiveness doesn't mean you have to let those people back into your life. Some doors need to stay closed for your protection. But you can still forgive from a distance. It's saying, *"I release you from my spirit. I release the hold you had on my peace."* And when you do that, something beautiful happens... you start to breathe again.

I remember the first time I realized I had truly forgiven. I saw the person who hurt me, and instead of anger, I felt peace. Not happiness, not joy, but peace. I didn't wish them harm. I didn't want revenge. I just wanted freedom. And that's when I knew — God had done the healing. Forgiveness doesn't erase the memory, but it removes the sting. You can remember what happened without reliving it.

## The Freedom in Forgiveness

Matthew 6:14–15 says: *"For if you forgive others their trespasses, your heavenly Father will also forgive you; but if you do not forgive others, neither will your Father forgive your trespasses."* Forgiveness isn't just a good idea — it's a divine command. God takes it seriously because He knows what it does to our hearts when we refuse to let go.

When you forgive, you open the door for God's blessings to flow again. Bitterness blocks blessings.

51

Unforgiveness clogs the spiritual arteries of your soul. But the moment you release it, peace comes rushing in like water over dry ground.

Some of the biggest breakthroughs in my life came right after I chose to forgive. I started sleeping better. My mind became clearer. I could worship freely again without heaviness sitting on my chest. That's the freedom that comes from letting go.

## A Heart Prayer for Forgiveness

If you're struggling to forgive right now — a parent, an ex, a friend, or even yourself — I want to invite you to pray this prayer with me:

*Lord, I'm tired of carrying this pain. I'm tired of replaying what they did. Today, I choose to*

*forgive. Not because they deserve it, but because I deserve peace.*

*I release them into Your hands, God. Heal my heart where it's been wounded.*

*Teach me to forgive like You forgive — fully, freely, and without limits. I release every hurt, every betrayal, and every unspoken pain.*

*Thank You for the freedom that comes through forgiveness. In Jesus' name, Amen.*

## Closing Reflection

Forgiveness isn't easy, but it's necessary. It's not a sign of weakness — it's proof of strength. It takes courage to let go of pain when holding on feels safer. But holding on keeps you bound to the past, while letting go opens your hands to receive what God has for your future.

When you choose forgiveness, you break the chains of bitterness, anger, and resentment that were keeping you tied to your past. You step into a new level of freedom, the kind that only God can give.

So, forgive. Not because they asked. Not because they deserve it. But because you deserve peace. Because at the end of the day, forgiveness isn't about forgetting what they did — it's about remembering what God did for you.

He forgave you, loved you, and gave you grace even when you didn't deserve it. And if He can forgive you, then surely you can forgive others. Forgiveness is the bridge between pain and peace. And once you cross it, that's when true inner healing begins.

Forgiveness opened a new chapter in my life, but it also revealed something deeper. Even after letting go of others, I still had to face the version of myself that was shaped by years of pain. Because sometimes, even when you've forgiven everyone else... the wounds still follow you.

## Closing Prayer

Lord, thank You for the freedom that comes when I choose to forgive. Give me the grace to release those who hurt me and the humility to forgive myself for staying too long.

Replace bitterness with peace and anger with compassion, and let forgiveness be the air I breathe. Teach me to walk in mercy the way You walk with me in mercy. In Jesus' name, Amen.

## Chapter Nine

### When the Wounds Follow You: My Journey into Adulthood

I used to believe that time alone would heal me. That if I stayed busy enough, smiled enough, and prayed enough, eventually the pain from my childhood would fade away on its own.

But pain you don't deal with doesn't disappear. It grows. It follows you into every new season of your life — into your friendships, your relationships, your parenting, and even into your faith.

I didn't realize it at the time, but the little girl who was hurt, silenced, and ashamed was still living inside of me. And because she was unhealed, she became the woman who didn't believe she was worthy of real love.

All the things I'd been through... the abuse, the shame, and the rejection had planted seeds of self-doubt deep inside me.

I told myself, *"I'm over it."* But I wasn't.

I told myself, *"I'm strong now."* But I was still

broken.

And because I never truly healed, I started making adult decisions with a wounded heart. I walked into relationships with a silent desperation to be loved, a desperation that made me ignore red flags, excuse bad behavior, and settle for treatment I didn't deserve.

I thought if I loved harder, prayed harder, or stayed longer, it would somehow heal me. But it didn't. Instead, it led me into one of the darkest seasons of my adult life.

## The Relationship That Broke Me

He came into my life like a calm breeze after a storm — charming, confident, and attentive. The kind of man who knew exactly what to say, how to make you feel seen, how to promise you things you've always longed to hear.

But slowly, the calm became chaos. The charm turned into control. And the control turned into abuse. What started with harsh words became manipulation. What began as jealousy turned into violence.

For five years, I stayed in a relationship with a man who beat me physically, emotionally, and spiritually. And the hardest truth to admit? I stayed because somewhere deep down, I thought that's what I deserved. When you grow up unhealed, pain starts to feel familiar, and familiarity can trick you into thinking it's love.

Looking back now, I can see how my unhealed trauma blinded me. When you've been taught to shrink

56

yourself to be loved, you start to accept crumbs as a feast. You start believing that love has to hurt.

**But love doesn't hurt; abuse does.**

## The Decision That Haunted Me

During that relationship, I became pregnant. And because my life felt like chaos, my heart was full of fear, and because I didn't believe I was worthy of anything good… I made a decision that still makes my heart ache to remember. I had an abortion. Even writing those words brings tears to my eyes. Not because God hasn't forgiven me, but because that decision became a turning point in my story. It was the moment I realized how far I had drifted from who I really was, from who God created me to be.

I made that choice out of fear, confusion, and deep self-hate. I didn't see any way out. And afterward, the shame felt unbearable. I carried it like a secret coat I couldn't take off. I thought, *"I'm too dirty. Too broken. Too far gone for God to love me now."*

But even then, in the middle of my guilt, in the middle of my self-loathing, grace was reaching for me. God's love met me in the very place I thought He would abandon me.

## The Mirror Moment

One night, after another fight, I sat on the cold bathroom floor with tears streaming down my face. My body was bruised. My spirit was shattered. My soul was tired. I looked up into the mirror and barely recognized the woman staring back at me. The little girl who once sang in church, who dreamed big dreams, who believed in love…she was gone. And that's when I heard it. A whisper. The same gentle voice that saved me when I was fourteen.

*"This is not who you are. Get up. Come back to Me."*

It wasn't loud, but it was enough. Enough to remind me that even though I had wandered far, I was never lost to God. Enough to show me that the same God who protected me as a little girl still had His hand on me as a broken woman. That whisper was my turning point.

Leaving wasn't easy. When you've been broken for so long, even freedom feels foreign. I prayed for change, but deep down I knew God was calling me to do something harder. He was calling me to walk away. My sister and her husband had just moved to Charlotte with their two children. She told me more than once, *"Whenever you're ready, you have a place here."*

For a long time, I ignored that lifeline, convincing myself that I could fix things. But one night, after another argument that left me trembling, I sat on the edge of my bed and whispered, *"Enough."*

That night, I told him calmly, "You have thirty days to find another place to live. I'm moving out." He laughed at first. He didn't believe me. He had broken me for so long that he didn't think I had any strength left to fight for myself. But what he didn't know was that God had already been rebuilding me piece by piece, strength by strength, prayer by prayer.

Those thirty days were long. I prayed through every sunrise and cried through every sunset. But underneath the fear, there was peace; the kind of peace that only comes when you've already decided to choose yourself.

When the day came, I packed my things, closed the door behind me, and didn't look back. As I drove to my sister's apartment in Charlotte, tears streamed down my face, tears of grief, of release, of relief. Every mile I drove felt like God was breaking a chain. When I pulled into my sister's driveway, she opened the door and wrapped her arms around me. Her husband welcomed me without judgment. For the first time in years, I felt safe.

That night, I lay awake staring at the ceiling, thinking about everything I had survived. I still felt fragile, but for the first time in a long time, I also felt hope. That move wasn't just a change of address. It was a change of identity. I was no longer the woman begging to be loved. I was the woman who finally believed she was worthy of love.

## Forgiving the Girl in the Mirror

Healing didn't just mean forgiving him, it also meant forgiving me… for the nights I stayed, for the lies I believed, for the abortion that haunted me. I stood in front of the mirror one day, looked myself in the eyes, and said out loud, "I forgive you. You did the best you could with what you knew."

And that moment was sacred. Because forgiveness opened the door for grace, and grace opened the door for healing. I realized I had spent so much time trying to protect myself that I had forgotten to let God protect me. When I finally handed my broken heart back to Him, He didn't shame me. He restored me.

## The Day I Chose Me

A few months later, I stood in church during worship, tears streaming down my face. The song was about freedom. As I lifted my hands, I felt something break off of me — the weight, the guilt, the shame. And in my spirit, I heard God whisper again, *"This time, you're really free."*

That was the day I realized healing isn't about forgetting the past; it's about no longer being chained to it. That day wasn't the end of my story, but it was the beginning of a new one. I walked out of that church knowing I would never again settle for pain disguised as love.

## Life After the Storm

The woman I am now still has scars, but they don't define me, they remind me. They remind me that

I survived. They remind me that grace found me in my darkest moments. When I look back now, I don't see a victim. I see a warrior who finally believed she was worth saving. I see a daughter of God who chose her own life.

Leaving that relationship was one of the hardest things I've ever done, but it also became one of the most defining. For the first time in my life, I chose peace over chaos. I chose to love myself enough to walk away.

But even after you escape the storm, you still have to learn how to live in the calm. Healing doesn't end when you leave what broke you. It begins when you start rebuilding what's left. And for me, that rebuilding began in marriage, a chapter that taught me that even love can be a classroom, and endings can still birth blessings.

## Closing Reflection

If you're in a place like I was, feeling stuck, afraid, or too broken to start over, please hear me: You can leave. You can heal. You can begin again. You may have to rebuild from the ground up, but God builds best on broken ground.

He is the same God who rescued me when I thought I was unworthy, and He will do the same for you. He will trade your chains for freedom. Your guilt for grace. Your ashes for beauty. You are not what happened to you. You are what you choose next.

**Closing Prayer**

Lord, thank You for meeting me in the places where my past tried to follow me. Heal the parts of me that still remember the pain and teach me to stop reliving old stories. Give me courage to protect my heart, to leave what is not from You, and to walk boldly into the freedom You've already given me. Help me to see myself the way You see me — whole, worthy, and loved. In Jesus' name, Amen.

## Chapter Ten
### Letting Go in Love: Finding Peace After Divorce

There was a time when I thought marriage alone could fix the broken places inside of me. I believed that if I loved hard enough, prayed enough, and gave all of myself, somehow everything would work out. But what I learned is that love alone isn't enough when two people are walking in different directions.

### The Blessing in the Breaking

My marriage lasted six years. It was full of ups and downs, laughter and tears, hope and heartbreak. We started with good intentions, two people trying to build a life together, but along the way, we lost sight of who we were as individuals and as a couple.

I tried to hold it together for as long as I could. I wanted so badly for it to work — not just for me, but for the picture I had in my mind of what a family "should" look like. But sometimes, God allows things to fall apart because He knows it's the only way we'll find ourselves again.

The divorce was painful. No one gets married thinking it will end. I remember sitting in court feeling a mix of sadness and relief, like I was watching the final scene of a story I once dreamed would last forever.

**But even in that pain, there was purpose.**

Out of that marriage came one of the greatest blessings of my life — my son. He is the light that came from a dark season, the proof that God can still bring beauty out of brokenness. When I look at him, I see strength, resilience, and unconditional love. He reminds me that even when relationships fail, God's promises don't.

At first, I struggled to see the blessing because I was so focused on the pain. But over time, I realized that my son was God's way of reminding me that even when life doesn't go as planned, He still has a plan. Divorce isn't just the separation of two people. It's the separation of dreams, habits, and the version of yourself you were in that relationship. For a long time, I wrestled with guilt. Guilt for the marriage not working. Guilt for walking away. Guilt for raising my son between two homes.

But through prayer and maturity, I learned that sometimes the healthiest thing you can do for your child is to create peace, even if that peace means being apart. We weren't good together as husband and wife, but we learned to be great together as co- parents.

At first, communication was hard. Emotions were still raw. But once we both decided that our son's happiness mattered more than our hurt, everything began to shift. Now, we talk with respect. We show up for him together. We celebrate his milestones without tension.

It's not perfect, but it is peaceful. And that's something I thank God for every day. It showed me that love doesn't have to disappear just because marriage ends, it just changes its form. The love we once had for each other transformed into a love for our child: selfless, unconditional, and grounded in peace.

## Finding Myself Again

After the divorce, I had to rediscover who I was outside of being someone's wife. I had to learn how to stand again — not just physically, but emotionally and spiritually. There were nights when loneliness crept in, and I questioned if I made the right decision. But God always found a way to remind me, peace is the confirmation that you're walking in the right direction.

In that quiet season, I started to fall back in love with myself. Not in a prideful way, but in a healing way. I started doing small things that made me happy again — going for walks, reading my Bible, laughing without fear of being silenced, and spending time with my son. Little by little, I started to feel like me again. Not the broken me. Not the wife trying to hold things together. But the woman God had been shaping all along.

## Lessons in Letting Go

Letting go after divorce isn't about pretending the marriage never happened — it's about accepting that it served its purpose. Some people come into our lives to teach us lessons, not to stay forever. And that's okay. That marriage taught me how to communicate, how to forgive, and how to set boundaries. It taught me that I can survive endings and still believe in love.

Most importantly, it taught me that I'm not defined by what didn't last — I'm defined by how I rise after it ends. Sometimes God allows us to lose something so we can gain something greater: peace, clarity, wisdom, and strength. Those are the gifts I carried out of that chapter.

## Moving Forward with Grace

Divorce taught me how to release what no longer serves me with grace instead of anger. It showed me that endings don't always mean failure, sometimes they mean freedom. I learned that I could love someone, forgive them, and still choose myself.

Letting go wasn't about hate; it was about healing. And even after everything, the pain, the disappointment, the fear of starting over, God still had a plan. Now, I can look back without resentment. I can say his name without bitterness.

I can even thank him in my prayers, because without that chapter, I wouldn't have my son, and I wouldn't be the woman I am today. That's what healing looks like, not forgetting but finding peace in what once hurt you.

Divorce didn't destroy me, it refined me. But even after the papers were signed and peace began to return, I realized something deeper: I was free on the outside, but still broken on the inside. And God wasn't content to leave me half-healed. He began to call me into a new kind of healing, the kind that doesn't just change your circumstances, but transforms your soul. It was time for redemption.

### Closing Reflection

Sometimes love stories don't end the way we imagine — but that doesn't mean they were a waste. My marriage taught me lessons that no classroom could. It showed me my strength, my patience, and my capacity for forgiveness.

And most of all, it gave me my son...my greatest gift. So, I choose to remember that chapter with gratitude, not regret. Because even though it ended, it helped me become the woman I am today — stronger, wiser, softer, and finally at peace.

## Closing Prayer

Lord, thank You for the grace to let go when love needs to change shape. Help me to walk in peace about the ending and to steward what remains — respect, maturity, and the bond of parenthood. Replace guilt with clarity, and help me to trust Your path forward. Teach me that endings can still hold blessings. In Jesus' name, Amen.

## Chapter Eleven
### Inner Healing: Redeemed and Whole Again

After the divorce, I realized that peace on the outside wasn't enough if I was still hurting on the inside. I had left a marriage, but I hadn't yet dealt with the emotions that came with it , the loss, the guilt, the loneliness, and the parts of myself I had buried just to survive.

That's when God began pulling me into something deeper, a season of inner healing. He wasn't just fixing my circumstances; He was mending my heart. As I learned to face my pain instead of running from it, I discovered that true freedom doesn't come from walking away. It comes from letting God walk you through.

Inner healing is finding freedom from emotional pain and the scars of the past. It's quiet, holy work, the kind that happens when you finally let God reach into the places you've tried to hide. It's not quick. It's not easy. But it's sacred.

## The Work of Healing

So many people think forgiveness is the end of

healing, but it's really just the beginning. Healing meant confronting the little girl in me who felt unworthy. The young woman who stayed too long in broken places. The mother who carried guilt for things she couldn't control. It meant tearing down walls I built to survive and letting God replace them with peace.

Some days, healing looked like worship and tears. Other days, it looked like counseling, journaling, and quiet drives talking to God. It wasn't always pretty. It was messy and uncomfortable — but it was worth it. Because every time I faced the pain, I found another piece of myself underneath it. And the deeper I allowed God to go, the freer I became.

After my divorce, I spent three and a half years single. At first, it felt like loneliness, but it became the most sacred time of my life. God wasn't punishing me; He was preparing me.

He rebuilt me from the inside out, teaching me discipline, showing me how to guard my peace, and reminding me that my identity was never tied to being someone's wife. In that quiet time, I began to love myself the way God loves me — fully, gently, and without conditions. And when I was ready, God whispered to my heart: *"You are ready."*

## The Drummer — A Love Story Written by God

There was a man at my church, the drummer. For more than a year, we passed each other in the hall, smiled, but never spoke. At the time, I didn't know God was keeping us silent for a reason.

He was working behind the scenes, healing both our hearts, aligning our timing, and preparing us for something real. When we finally did speak, it wasn't fireworks. It was peace. Our friendship grew naturally. We prayed together. We laughed together. We shared our stories without fear or judgment.

He didn't just hear my story, he honored it. He didn't try to fix my past. He respected the woman it shaped me to be. That's how I knew this love was different.

## A Love Redeemed

Today, I'm married to that man, the drummer who once stood in the background but is now the steady rhythm of my life. He didn't replace my past; he redeemed it. He showed me that love can be gentle, safe, and rooted in God's timing. He has a son who's seven now, and our boys are the best of friends. Watching them play and grow together feels like watching God weave two stories into one.

Now, my husband and I serve together in ministry, not just as a couple, but as partners in purpose. Every Sunday, when I see him behind the drums and our boys smiling in the front row, I'm reminded: God's timing is perfect.

This love feels different. Not because it's perfect, but because it's purposeful. It's laughter after pain, peace after chaos, and faith after fear. He covers me in prayer, encourages my calling, and loves me without condition.

This love isn't my reward for surviving, it's the reflection of God's redemption. And the best part? I didn't have to chase it. It found me when I finally became the woman who knew she deserved it.

Healing taught me that I didn't need someone to complete me; I needed God to make me whole. When you heal, you no longer crave love from emptiness; you love from overflow. Now, I see that every heartbreak, every tear, every lonely night wasn't wasted. They were all part of the refining, the preparation for this peace. My past didn't disqualify me, it prepared me. Redeemed, Restored, and Ready

When I look at my life now, I don't just see healing. I see redemption. I see a woman who once thought she'd never love again, now waking up beside a man who prays over her. I see two boys growing in love and laughter. I see purpose rising from pain. Every chapter, the trauma, the divorce, the waiting... led me here. To a season where I can finally say, *"I am whole."*

## Closing Reflection

When I look back over my life, I see a story only God could write. The girl who once felt unworthy now walks in her purpose.

The woman who thought she'd never love again is loved beyond measure. And the mother who once prayed for strength now wakes up every day surrounded by grace. I am not who I used to be. I am who God always knew I could become. I am healed.

I am whole.

I am redeemed.

And I am free.

Rodlyn Wilson

## Closing Prayer

Lord, thank You for the beauty that comes after breaking and the love that comes after healing. Thank You for writing a story of redemption that only You could create. Keep my heart soft, my spirit humble, and my eyes focused on You. Let my testimony be proof that nothing is beyond Your reach and that restoration is real. In Jesus' name, Amen.

# Final Reflection: The Beautiful Face

I used to think beauty meant perfection. Now I know beauty means survival, truth, and grace. The ugly truth was never about my face; it was about my heart. And the beautiful face was never about appearance, it was about transformation. I am living proof that God still heals, still restores, and still rewrites stories. And if He did it for me, He can do it for you.

**Final Prayer**

Lord, thank You for every chapter of my life — the broken ones, the beautiful ones, and the ones still being written. Thank You for turning pain into purpose and wounds into wisdom. May my story reach every heart that feels unseen and remind them that Your love is still enough. Let healing flow through these pages and hope rise in every reader. In Jesus' name, Amen.

# Author Bio

My name is Rodlyn Wilson, and my life is a story of grace, growth, and new beginnings. I am 38 and recently married to the love of my life. I am a proud mother to a wonderful son and a grateful stepmother to an amazing stepson. Our blended family reminds me every day that God restores what we surrender and multiplies it with love.

I have worked in banking for more than ten years and I currently serve at the United States Senate Federal Credit Union. My career has taught me patience, excellence, and the joy of serving people well. I believe service is ministry in motion, and I carry that heart into everything I do.

I am a minister who loves the presence of God and the healing that comes through worship. I serve as a liturgical praise dancer, using movement to pray, to testify, and to create space for others to feel God's nearness. I am also a praise team leader at my church, where I help usher people into worship and encourage hearts to lift their voices with faith and expectation.

Beyond ministry and banking, I am a motivational speaker and a certified life coach. I love to inspire people to rise after hard seasons, to forgive themselves, and to believe that purpose still lives within them. Writing is another part of my calling. I write from a place of honesty and hope, inviting readers to see that every chapter has meaning. I have known the pain of divorce and the beauty of restoration. I have learned that nothing is wasted when placed in God's hands. Today I stand as a wife, a mother, a minister, a dancer, a leader, a banker, a coach, and a writer, grateful for the journey and excited for all that is still to come.

www.ingramcontent.com/pod-product-compliance
Lightning Source LLC
Chambersburg PA
CBHW061713120626
46550CB00003B/1206